YOU CAN HEAR GOD'S VOICE

STUDY GUIDE

BY
DR. KEVIN L. ZADAI

Dedication

I dedicate this book to the Lord Jesus Christ. When I died during surgery and met with Jesus on the other side, He insisted that I return to life on the earth and that I help people with their destinies. Because of Jesus' love and concern for people, the Lord has actually chosen to send a person back from death to help everyone who will receive that help so that his or her destiny and purpose is secure in Him. I want You, Lord, to know that when You come to take me to be with You someday, it is my sincere hope that people remember not me, but the revelation of Jesus Christ that You have revealed through me. I want others to know that I am merely being obedient to Your heavenly calling and mission, which is to reveal Your plan for the fulfillment of the divine destiny for each of God's children.

Acknowledgments

In addition to sharing my story with everyone through the books *Heavenly Visitation: A Guide to the Supernatural, Days of Heaven on Earth: A Guide to the Days Ahead, A Meeting Place with God, Your Hidden Destiny Revealed, Praying from the Heavenly Realms: Supernatural Secrets to a Lifestyle of Answered Prayer, The Agenda of Angels, and Supernatural Finances,* the Lord gave me a commission to produce this book, *You Can Hear God's Voice.* This book addresses some of the revelations concerning the areas that Jesus reviewed and revealed to me through the Word of God and by the Spirit of God during several visitations. I want to thank everyone who has encouraged me, assisted me and prayed for me during the writing of this work, especially my spiritual parents, Dr. Jesse Duplantis, and Dr. Cathy Duplantis. Special thanks to my wonderful wife Kathi for her love and dedication to the Lord and to me. Thanks to my awesome staff for their work on the editing of this book. Thank you, Destiny Image and staff, for your support. Thank you, Sid Roth and staff, for your love of our supernatural Messiah, Jesus. Special thanks to all my friends who know *You Can Hear God's Voice* and how to operate in this for the next move of God's Spirit!

DR. KEVIN L. ZADAI

Contents

DR. KEVIN L. ZADAI

Introduction

What is the greatest desires of my heart, throughout my life, was to hear God's voice. As I travel the world, I found this to be true everywhere. After encountering Jesus in 1992, I discovered that ***GOD DESIRES FOR YOU TO HEAR HIS VOICE!*** In this amazing study guide, you will learn the following:

- How to access your rights and privileges as a believer who is created in the image of God.
- Learn to recognize God's voice through intimate fellowship in prayer and meditation.
- How to walk-in increased discernment through the Holy Spirit's power.
- Encounter new clarity in your ability to know the will of God.
- Walk in total transformation through the renewing of your mind.

I have learned from Jesus that you can walk with God and hear His voice. It is time to gain understanding concerning the truth that God want you to fellowship with Him.

Dr. Kevin L. Zadai

DR. KEVIN L. ZADAI

CHAPTER 1

Created in His Image

"So God created man in His image; in the image of God He created him; male and female He created them." Genesis 1:27

DISCUSSION:

God created you to have fellowship with Him, and He wants to speak to you. He also wants you to hear His voice. God has sent the Holy Spirit here to talk with you and help you. The Holy Spirit is your counselor, guide, advocate, minister, teacher, and comforter. Do not ever doubt that God wants you to hear His voice. You can develop your spirit and increase your ability to hear God's voice. In this earth realm, it is possible to hear many kinds of voices. You can hear voices from your body, from your soul and the spirit realm for good or evil. You must be aware that demonic activity can deceive you so you must be careful. You must always be reading the Word of God and meditating on it to strengthen your belief system and your spirit. You must also pray in the spirit, in tongues to build yourself up (see Jude 20). If you are not baptized in the Holy Spirit, you need to be instructed in this and yield to the Spirit of God. And they were all filled with the Holy Spirit and began to speak with other tongues, as the Spirit gave them utterance (Acts 2:4). The bible clearly teaches that tongues are for today.

❖ **2 Corinthians 5:17** "Therefore, if anyone is in Christ, he is a new creation; old things have passed away; behold, all things have become new."

- One of the things necessary to hear God's voice is to be born again of the Spirit of God.

- Becoming born again happens when you ask Jesus to come into your heart, you give your life over to Him, and you are born again (see John 3:3).
- You need to express your faith in Jesus, the Son of God, who died for your sins. You must believe that Jesus died, was buried, rose from the dead, and ascended to the right hand of the Father in Heaven.

- When you accept Jesus into your heart, the Holy Spirit will come into your life. The Holy Spirit will change your heart, and you will know that your sins are forgiven. You will truly be a new creation in Christ Jesus.
- When you are born again, old things have passed away, but you must still live out your life on this earth. God wants you to find out what He has done for you through His Son Jesus Christ. You must always be seeking and pursuing God and His Word.

What happens when you regularly read the Word of God and meditate on it?

_____

_____

_____

_____

_____

- ❖ **<u>Hebrews 11:6</u>** "But without faith it is impossible to please Him, for He who comes to God must believe that He is, and that He is a rewarder of those who diligently seek Him."

  - God rewards you when you diligently seek Him.

- When you are born again, the power of God comes into your heart.
- The Holy Spirit is the one who caused you to be born again.
- The Holy Spirit causes your spirit to change into a new creation.
- Now you are equipped to hear God's voice.
- Everyone that is born again by the Spirit of God can hear God's voice.
- Some children of God have not been able to hear God's voice because we live in a fallen realm.
- Many do not know the Word of God and have not built themselves up in their most holy faith.
- They may not be baptized in the Holy Spirit and do not pray in tongues.
- They cannot hear God's voice even though He is speaking to them.

What equips you to hear the voice of God?

_____

_____

_____

_____

_____

_____

- ❖ **Genesis 1:26-28** "Then God said, 'Let us make man in Our image, according to Our likeness; let them have dominion over the fish of the sea, over the birds of the air, and over the cattle, over all the earth and over every creeping thing that creeps on the earth.' So God created man in His own image; in the image of God He created him; male and female He created them. Then God blessed them, and God said to them, 'Be fruitful and multiply; fill the earth and subdue it; have dominion over the fish of the sea, over the birds of the air, and over every living thing that moves on the earth.'"

- "Let *us* make man in our image," the plural us, represents the Holy Trinity: Father, Son, and Holy Spirit.
- God's original intent for man was to have a creation that not only looked like Him but was also like Him in many ways. God wanted someone to talk to and have communion and fellowship with, and that was why He made man.
- God would come down in the cool of the day and visit with Adam and Eve in the garden and walk with them (see Genesis 3:8).
- When lucifer saw the close and intimate relationship that God had with Adam and Eve in the garden, he became jealous.
- The fall of man was initiated by a jealous cherub, lucifer, working through the serpent.
- Adam and Eve became separated from God and lost their relationship with Him (See Genesis 3).

DISCUSSION:

Jesus came back to redeem us, who are made in God's image and restore us once again to God in the born again, experience. Through Christ, we have an even greater covenant with even greater promises from God. We are made in the image of God, and we have the voice of God inside of our spirit when we are born again. In God's image, we can speak, we can reason, hear, see, make decisions, and converse. In His image, we can listen to God, and He can listen to us, and we can talk with God. We can walk with God, and He can walk with us.

GROWTH IN CHRIST

- ❖ **2 Peter 1:4** "By which have been given to us exceedingly great and precious promises, that through these you may be partakers of the divine nature, having escaped the corruption that is in the world through lust."

- You can be a partaker of the divine nature through God's promises.
- You have been restored to the Father, and you are a child of God.
- You have a Father who loves you and wants to talk to you and commune with you and spend time with you.

- ❖ **Luke 10:19** "Behold, I give you the authority to trample on serpents and scorpions, and over all the power of the enemy, and nothing shall by any means hurt you."

  - Jesus restored the authority given to us by God.
  - You are born again, redeemed and your dominion reestablished through Jesus Christ's death and resurrection.
  - You can experience deliverance personally.
  - When you administer your authority, you have dominion over serpents, scorpions, and over all the power of the enemy.

In what area of your life is the Holy Spirit showing you that you need to take authority over?

_____

_____

_____

_____

_____

_____

- ❖ **Matthew 3:13-17** "Then Jesus came from Galilee to John at the Jordan to be baptized by him. And John tried to prevent Him, saying, 'I need to be baptized by You, and are You coming to me?' But Jesus answered and said to him, 'Permit it to be so now, for thus it is fitting for us to fulfill all righteousness.' Then he allowed Him. When He had been baptized, Jesus came up immediately from the water; and behold, the Heavens were opened to Him, and He saw the Spirit of God descending like a dove and alighting upon Him. And suddenly a voice came from Heaven, saying, 'This is My beloved Son, in whom I am well pleased.'"

- The account of Jesus baptism tells how the Father, Son, and Holy Spirit appeared together in the same place.
- Another time that the Trinity appears together happens in Genesis 1:26, when God says, "Let us make man in Our image."
- To be able to hear from God, it is important to establish these facts about the Holy Trinity.
- There are many more dimensions in the spirit realm than in the earth realm.
- The Holy Trinity is three persons in one, and they are all in your life.

❖ **God the Father can speak to you, God the Son can speak to you and God the Holy Spirit can speak to you and reveal themselves to you.**

❖ **The Father has done all this for us. Jesus came and restored to the Father His creation called man.**

❖ **We are redeemed through the blood of Jesus, and now everyone can come to God, believe, and be saved.**

Do you consistently find yourself drawn to only one person of the Holy Trinity? Reflect on what could be stopping you from having a relationship with *each* person of the Holy Trinity?

_____

_____

_____

_____

_____

❖ **Revelation 13:8** "And all who dwell on the earth will worship him, whose names have not been written in the Book of Life of the Lamb slain from the foundation of the world."

- Even though everyone has been redeemed from the foundation of the world, people still go to hell.
- They did not acknowledge Jesus as their Savior.
- You need to hear God's voice and know God's plan for your life.
- Then you need to go out and tell people that they have been forgiven of their sins. You need to tell them to repent of their sins, ask God for forgiveness, and they will be saved.

❖ **Isaiah 46:9-10** "Remember the former things of old, for I am God, and there is no other; I am God, and there is none like Me, declaring the end from the beginning, and from ancient times things that are not yet done, saying, 'My counsel shall stand, and I will do all My pleasure.'"

- God already knows everything. He declares the end from the beginning things that are not yet done.

- His pleasure was that He designed this plan of redemption through Jesus Christ slain from the foundation of the world.
- Each of your days was written in a book before one of them came to be (see Psalms 139:16).
- God saw your body being formed in your mother's womb, and He knew you long before you were ever born.

DISCUSSION:

The Holy Trinity knew everything before it happened. God has already known every moment of your life. God has given you a will and your will, emotions, mind, and the way that you reason can work against God or work with God. Your understanding of this will have a lot to do with hearing God's voice. The Apostle Paul talked about the fact that he had killed Christians and had done all sorts of terrible things, yet he said that he was set apart as an apostle from birth. Paul had received the revelation that God foreknew everything about him. God knew in advance that Paul would be an apostle and do amazing things for the kingdom of God. Do not worry about things that have already happened in your life; God has taken care of all that through Jesus Christ's death and resurrection. Concentrate on what is ahead for you and the plan that God has for your life.

Is the Holy Spirit showing you any part of your soul—your mind, will, emotions, or reasoning that have been working against God's purposes in your life?

_____

_____

_____

_____

_____

_____

CHAPTER 2

You Have Been Predestined

"But I make known to you, brethren, that the gospel which was preached by me is not according to man. For I neither received it from man, nor was I taught it, but it came through the revelation of Jesus Christ." Galatians 1:11-12

❖ **Galatians 1:13-17** "For you have heard of my former conduct in Judaism, how I persecuted the church of God beyond measure and tried to destroy it. And I advanced in Judaism beyond many of my contemporaries in my own nation, being more exceedingly zealous for the traditions of my fathers. But when it pleased God, who separated me from my mother's womb and called me through His grace, to reveal His Son to me, that I might preach Him among the Gentiles, I did not immediately confer with flesh and blood, nor did I go up to Jerusalem to those who were apostles before me; but I went to Arabia and returned again to Damascus."

DISCUSSION:

Paul said that he was foreordained from his mother's womb by God to be an apostle. Jesus Christ revealed Himself to Paul and then through Paul to the Gentiles. Even though Paul was separated out from his birth to be an apostle, in the early part of his life, he was persecuting and killing Christians and trying to destroy the church. Paul believed that he was working for God, but he was really working against the purposes of God. Jesus arrested Paul on the road to Damascus, where Paul met Jesus face to face, and his life was forever turned around (see Acts 9:4-9). Jesus called

Paul, at that time, but his real call and purpose were written before he was ever born. It is the same for us today, God in His foreknowledge knows everything about us, and He has a plan for each one of us. However, our mind, will and emotions, our soul part can cause us to work contrary to the plan of God in our lives. Even though God knows the future, He will never try to control or manipulate us or make us do anything. People go to hell because they reject Jesus or they are not told about Him, or they will refuse to acknowledge Him. We need to preach the gospel of Jesus Christ to everyone and tell them that they are redeemed by the blood of the Lamb (see 2 Corinthians 17-21).

❖ **God wanted a family, so He purchased us back before we were ever born.**

God has a plan for your life, and it includes sharing the gospel of Jesus Christ. What has been stopping you or limiting you from sharing Christ with others?

_____

_____

_____

_____

_____

_____

CHOSEN BY THE FATHER

❖ **Ephesians 1:3-12** "Blessed be the God and Father of our Lord Jesus Christ, who has blessed us with every spiritual blessing in the Heavenly places in Christ, just as He chose us in Him before the foundation of the world, that we should be holy and without blame before Him in love, having predestined us to adoption as sons of Jesus Christ to Himself, according to the good pleasure of His will, to the praise of the glory of His grace by which He has made us accepted in the Beloved. In Him we have redemption through His blood, the forgiveness of sins, according to the riches of His grace which He made to abound toward us in all wisdom and prudence, having made known to us the mystery of His will, according to His good pleasure which He purposed in Himself, that in the dispensation of the fullness of the times He might gather together in one all things in Christ, both which are in Heaven and which are on earth-in Him, in whom also we have obtained an inheritance, being predestined according to the purpose of Him who works all things according to the counsel of His will, that we who first trusted in Christ should be to the praise of His glory."

- God has already blessed you with every spiritual blessing in the Heavenly places in Christ; it has already happened.
- Concentrate on renewing and transforming your mind.
- God chose you in Him before the foundation of the world.
- God loves you, and you are His child.
- You are holy and without blame before Him in love, accept that your blame has been taken away.
- You have already been determined to be adopted into the Sonship.
- You have been accepted into the Beloved long before you were born.
- He has made known to you the mystery of His will.

❖ **When you give yourself over to God and bend your will to Him, you will see that you are in the family of God in Heaven and on the earth.**

❖ **You have a direct line of communication in your spirit to God; part of the Holy Trinity is inside of you.**

❖ **You can now participate in the fullness of God, and you can hear His voice.**

- ❖ **2 Corinthians 4:3-4** "But even if our gospel is veiled, it is veiled to those who are perishing, whose mind the god of this world has blinded, who do not believe, lest the light of the gospel of the glory of Christ, who is the image of God, should shine on them."

  - The god of this world, satan, has blinded the minds of those who don't believe.
  - Those who do not believe cannot see the glorious light of the good news.
  - Jesus Christ is the exact image of the Father, and you were created in their image.
  - "Then God said, 'Let Us make man in Our image, according to Our likeness (Genesis 1:26).'"
  - When you receive Jesus, you receive the Holy Spirit.
  - The Holy Spirit leads you to the Father.

- ❖ **Jesus came to earth in a body in the image of man, but He was God.**

- ❖ **Jesus was pre-existent, and He was sent into flesh.**

- ❖ **Jesus walked among us as Immanuel, and He manifested God to us as a servant.**

- ❖ **Jesus showed us how to live on earth as a man with God in Him.**

- ❖ **Jesus lived His life on earth as the Father wants us to live our lives.**

- ❖ **Jesus was crucified for us; He took our place to restore us back to the Father.**

What can you expect to happen when you give yourself over to God and bend your will to His?

_____

_____

_____

_____

_____

_____

❖ **1 John 3:2-3** "Beloved, now we are children of God; and it has not yet been revealed what we shall be, but we know that when He is revealed, we shall be like Him, for we shall see Him as He is. And everyone who has this hope in Him purifies himself, just as He is pure. We do look like Jesus, and we will see Him as He is."

❖ **Ephesians 5:1-2** "Therefore be imitators of God as dear children. And walk in love, as Christ also has loved us and given Himself for us, an offering and a sacrifice to God for a sweet-smelling aroma."

- As children imitate their parents, we are to imitate God as His dear children.
- We are to want to grow up and be like our Father in Heaven and enjoy fellowship with Him.
- God has restored us back, and now He wants to talk to us face to face.
- Moses was so transformed after forty days on the mountain with God that his face shone, and the Israelites feared him (see Exodus 34:29).
- Moses was being restored to what Adam originally looked like in the garden.

❖ **Genesis 1:26** "Then God said, 'Let Us make man in Our image, according to Our likeness; let them have dominion over the fish of the sea, over the birds of the air, and over the cattle, over all the earth and over every creeping thing that creeps on the earth.'"

- God gave Adam and Eve dominion over these sectors—the sea, the air, and the ground.
- God redeemed man through His Son Jesus Christ, and it is through our redemption that we have dominion and authority over satanic forces.
- We have authority over fallen angels and evil spirits that roam the earth. They are under our feet as born again believers.

DISCUSSION:

The fact has been established that God had a plan for us long before we were ever born. He has brought us back from sin and death and has redeemed us. Now He is asking us to be imitators of God as dearly beloved children. God is full of authority and dominion, and He gave Adam and Eve dominion over all the earth, the sea, air, and ground. Through Jesus Christ, God has given us dominion over satanic forces. Our authority is over evil spirits, and they have been put under our feet.

What are some ways that you can imitate your beloved Heavenly Father?

_____

_____

_____

_____

_____

_____

_____

❖ **Hebrews 2:5-9** "For He has not put the world to come, of which we speak, in subjection to angels. But one testified in a certain place, saying: 'What is man that You are mindful of him, Or the son of man that You take care of him? You made him a little lower than the angels; You have crowned him with glory and honor, And set him over the works of Your hands. You have put all things in subjection under his feet.' For in that He put all in subjection under him, He left nothing that is not put under Him. But now we do not yet see all things put under him. But we see Jesus, who was made a little lower than the angels, for the suffering of death crowned with glory and honor, that He, by the grace of God, might taste death for everyone."

- Jesus came and took our place on the cross and bought us back.
- Everything is in subjection under Jesus' feet.
- We are the body of Christ, and He is our head.
- Through the church and the body of Christ, we have dominion over everything.
- When you know who you are in Christ and use your God-given authority demon spirits know it too.
- Jesus is our focus until everything comes into the millennial reign and is put under Him.

DISCUSSION:

God commanded the blessing over Adam and Eve and for all mankind. God told them to participate in their dominion of the earth. Adam named all the animals on the earth, and they are named until this day. The Holy Trinity gave Adam and Eve dominion and authority over all the earth. God spoke over them to be fruitful and multiply. As a human being living on the earth, we feel the power, ability, and passion for being fruitful and multiplying, it is part of who we are. God wants us to fill the earth and populate it. Be mindful that God has more for you and has put more in you than you realize. God has been speaking to you to be fruitful and multiply.

What is God speaking to you about being fruitful and multiplying?

_____

_____

_____

_____

_____

_____

_____

_____

_____

_____

_____

CHAPTER 3

Dominion and Authority

"Then God blessed them, and God said to them, 'Be fruitful and multiply; fill the earth and subdue it; have dominion over the fish of the sea, over the birds of the air, and over every living thing that moves on the earth.'" Genesis 1:28

DISCUSSION:

God spoke a blessing over mankind. He commanded man to be fruitful, multiply, fill the earth, and subdue it. Dominion is part of God's kingdom, and God made dominion part of man. God has placed in man the desire to have dominion and be fruitful. When we have no plan or purpose for our life, we feel frustrated because God has already spoken over us to do these things. When you are full of the world and not born again, the spirit of this world, the devil controls you. He causes you to be unfruitful, not able to multiply, and he causes you to have no purpose. You are unable to follow the plan of God for your life. When you are born again, you receive knowledge and wisdom, and your spirit is lit up by the Holy Spirit within you. You will want to subdue and have dominion over evil spirits, and as a Christian, it is within you to do just that. God told man to subdue the earth; the word subdue is a strong military term. Subdue in Hebrew means to tread down, to conquer, to force or to bring under submission. It is within you to do this because it was spoken over man by God. God wants us to gather, replenish, set apart, and subdue the earth, and then He wants us to propagate and fill the earth. God trusted Adam to name all the animals on the earth, and Adam was given the authority to be in charge of all the earth. When man fell in the garden, Adam gave his God-given authority over the earth to satan. Sin now separated man from God, and Adam and Eve had to leave the garden. When Jesus redeemed mankind back to the Father, man was now restored in the dominion and authority of God once again. So much more has been given to you through Jesus Christ than you know.

❖ **Matthew 11:11-15** "Assuredly, I say to you, among those born of women there has not risen one greater than John the Baptist; but he who is least in the kingdom of Heaven is greater than he. And from the days of John the Baptist until now the kingdom of Heaven suffers violence, and the violent take it by force. For all the prophets and the law prophesied until John. And if you are willing to receive it, He is Elijah who is to come. He who has ears to hear, let him hear!"

- No one before John the Baptist was greater than John, and he is the least in the kingdom of God from his day until now.
- If you want to hear the voice of God, you must realize what Jesus has invested in you.
- You are greater than anyone who has come before you, the least from now on is greater than John the Baptist.
- The power of God is resting on you in this time, and this age and He wants you to speak the word of God with signs and wonders following for confirmation.
- God wants to pour out His Spirit and show His glory to the people of the earth.
- The kingdom of God is advancing.
- You, as a born again child of the kingdom of God, are participating in the supernatural power of God.

❖ **Mark 16:16-18** "He who believes and is baptized will be saved; but he who does not believe will be condemned. And these signs will follow those who believe; In My name they will cast out demons; they will speak with new tongues; they will take up serpents; and if they drink anything deadly, it will by no means hurt them; they will lay hands on the sick, and they will recover."

- John the Baptist had no recorded miracles in his ministry; his one message was repentance.
- We now have the revelation from sixty-six books of the Bible, and we can preach the gospel of Jesus Christ in all the earth.
- When we preach the gospel these signs will follow, the sick will be healed, demons will be cast out, the dead will be raised, and we will speak with new tongues.

When you apply the kingdom truth that the least in the kingdom of God is now greater than John the Baptist, what can you expect to see when you preach the gospel of Jesus Christ?

_____

_____

_____

_____

_____

_____

GOD'S COVENANT WITH MOSES

❖ **Genesis 9:1-4** "So God blessed Noah and his sons, and said to them: 'Be fruitful and multiply, and fill the earth. And the fear of you and the dread of you shall be on every beast of the earth, on every bird of the air, on all that move on the earth, and on all the fish of the sea. They are given into your hand. Every moving thing that lives shall be food for you. I have given you all things, even as the green herbs. But you shall not eat the flesh with its life, that is, its blood.'"

- God is repeating His command to Noah and his sons to be fruitful and multiply.
- Gods dominion principle still stands.

Why is it significant that God repeats His blessing from Genesis 1 over Noah and his sons?

_____

_____

_____

_____

_____

_____

REVIEW

- **We were created in God's image.**
- **We not only look like God; we are also like God.**
- **The blessing of God spoken over us is to be fruitful and multiply.**
- **God commands us to fill the earth, subdue it, and have dominion over it.**
- **It is in us to rule and reign, and it is not in us to be slaves.**
- **God never intended His children to be slaves.**
- **Jesus Christ redeemed us, pulled us out of sin, and washed us in His blood.**
- **We are seated with Jesus in the Heavenly realms (see Ephesians 2:6).**
- **We were made to have dominion and authority.**

- Adam named the animals what *he* determined to name them.
- We must start to rule and reign.
- God's plans and purposes for us is to dominate, to be the children of God who have inherited all that the kingdom of Heaven offers.
- You must be disciplined in your life, saying no to ungodliness and worldly passions.
- You must live an upright life in Christ Jesus, saying no to the flesh.
- You must not fear because you are a child of God bought with a great price.
- Jesus purchased you, redeemed you, and set you back in authority.
- You have been restored back to God's original plan for man in kingdom authority.
- The demons that have stopped you from hearing from God will now begin to flee.
- God made you in His image, and He made you to dominate.

In what ways is the Holy Spirit speaking to you regarding being more disciplined in your life and saying no to ungodliness and worldly passions?

_____

_____

_____

_____

_____

_____

_____

_____

_____

DISCUSSION:

You can now see that you are made in God's image, and He created you to dominate. He made you to rule and reign and have authority. In your spirit, you know this, but in your mind, you may be hearing the opposite. Evil spirits can work on you to keep you in a small place, but God never intended man to live this way. When Jesus came and redeemed us, He conquered death, hell, and the grave. He defeated satan, disarmed him, and made a show of those evil spirits openly (see Colossians 2:15). The Apostle Paul had this revelation of dominion from Heaven that evil spirits must listen to you. When you command someone to come back from the dead, you will raise the dead. You will heal the sick, and when you say, "Sickness go!" evil spirits will have to go. You have dominion over serpents, scorpions, and demons, and they must obey you in Jesus' name. The reason why you may not hear God's voice is that you are in warfare. Take authority and dominion over every evil spirit in your life. There are evil spirits that follow your bloodline called familiar spirits. You have to break the power of these curses in your family in Jesus' name. You need to take your God-given authority and drive them out in Jesus' name, and they have to listen to you and obey

❖ <u>**2 Corinthians 10:4-5**</u> "For the weapons of our warfare are not carnal but mighty in God for the pulling down of strongholds, casting down arguments and every high thing that exalts itself against the knowledge of God, bringing every thought into captivity to the obedience of Christ."

- The above Scripture is very powerful, and it is where warfare happens.
- You must be rough and forceful with the devil.
- God intended you to dominate the devil, not for the devil to dominate you.
- You need to pull down strongholds in prayer.
- Cast down arguments and every high thing that exalts itself against the knowledge of God.
- Anything that is saying the opposite to the Word of God in your life, you must come against it now in Jesus' name.

- ❖ Jesus came in the image of man, but He was God, and He redeemed you back to the Father and restored you.
- ❖ It is in you to rule and reign. You have dominion power and authority, and you must acknowledge God in all your ways.
- ❖ God knows your name, and He has written a wonderful book about you. God can accomplish anything in your life, and nothing is impossible.
- ❖ Your life is different now because God will intervene in your life, and all limitations have been taken off.
- ❖ Demonic spirits will not hinder you anymore because you know how to take dominion, power, and authority.

The voice of God is speaking to you right now about how you can pull down strongholds in prayer. Take a moment and let the Holy Spirit lead you into an authoritative prayer; take your dominion over the enemy, in Jesus' name.

_____

_____

_____

_____

_____

_____

THE DOMINION PRINCIPLE

The dominion principle is this, God's kingdom will rule forever and ever. God is seated on His throne, and He will never leave it or be defeated. You as His child will never be defeated; you are more than a conqueror (see Romans 8:37), and you are made in God's image. You were designed to rule and reign. The voice of God may have been obscured in your life because you have been in warfare with satan. He can surround you and keep God's voice from being the loudest voice in your life. You must start weeding out the voices in your life that speak louder than God. It is a process where you must yield dominion over yourself to Father God, Jesus the Son and the Holy Spirit and come under their authority. Jesus said to take His yoke upon you, and it is easy, and His burden is light (see Matthew 11:30). All demons will know when you walk in the authority of God and His dominion. Ask the Holy Spirit to cleanse you and remove the things in your life that are not of God.

❖ **Hebrews 4:12** "For the word of God is living and powerful, and sharper than any two-edged sword, piercing even to the division of soul and spirit, and of joints and marrow, and is a discerner of the thoughts and intents of the heart."

- When you are born again, the sword of the word of God separates between your soul; your mind, will, emotions, and your spirit.
- The voice of your spirit must be louder than your soul nature.
- The word of God will tell you what is of your spirit and what is of your soul.
- Hearing the voice of God will become easier as you allow God's authority and dominion in your life to rule over you. You will begin to hear God's voice louder and louder in your life.
- Through this process, you will start to rule and reign and have dominion and authority.

What are the voices in your life speaking louder than the voice of God? Repent from your role in listening and ask the Holy Spirit to help you to quiet them.

_____

_____

_____

_____

_____

_____

- ❖ You are crucified with Christ do not live your life for yourself anymore.

- ❖ "I assure you, believers, by the pride which I have in you in [your union with] Christ Jesus our Lord, I die daily [I face death and die to self] (1 Corinthians 15:31 AMP)."

- ❖ The Apostle Paul said that he died daily, and you must practice this too.

- ❖ Yield to the yoke of God and say, not my will but Yours be done and let Jesus show you how to walk in the Holy Spirit.

- ❖ Say "no" to the flesh and say "yes" to the Holy Spirit of God.

- ❖ The Spirit of God that is in you will lead you into all truth.

What does it mean to be crucified with Christ and die daily?

_____

_____

_____

_____

_____

_____

_____

_____

DR. KEVIN L. ZADAI

CHAPTER 4

The Role of the Holy Spirit

"Now may the God of peace Himself sanctify you completely;
and may your whole spirit, soul and body be preserved blameless at the coming of
our Lord Jesus Christ." 1 Thessalonians 5:23

DISCUSSION:

When you want to hear God's voice, you must remember that God is a Spirit. God is going to speak with you in a spiritual sense. There are three parts of man; you have a spirit, a soul, and a body. "God is Spirit, and those who worship Him must worship in spirit and truth (John 4:24)." "Now the Lord is the Spirit; and where the Spirit of the Lord *is*, there is liberty (2 Corinthians 3:17)." The Holy Spirit dwells inside of you, and when God speaks with you, it is Spirit-to-spirit. God brings you up into His realm. Once you understand these principles, you can discern God's voice because it is often a still small voice that comes into your spirit.

❖ **Genesis 1:1-2** "In the beginning God created the Heavens and the earth. The earth was without form, and void; and darkness was on the face of the deep. And the Spirit of God was hovering over the face of the waters."

- In this Scripture, the Holy Trinity is working together to form creation.
- The Holy Spirit was in a standby position hovering over the face of the deep.
- The Holy Spirit was there to execute all the commands that the Father was speaking.

- God framed the world with His Word; everything was created through Jesus Christ.
- The Holy Spirit was active over all creation, monitoring it, an advocate, a standby, and He executed the Word of God.
- The Holy Spirit in you comforts you in these same ways. He is on standby for you.
- When God speaks or sings over you, even in your sleep, the Holy Spirit is awake and active.
- "The Lord your God in your midst, The Mighty One, will save; He will rejoice over you with gladness, He will quiet you with His love, He will rejoice over you with singing (Zephaniah 3:17)."
- God wants to speak to you all the time, even in your dreams. He speaks to your inner man, a spiritual voice inside of you, giving you information from Heaven.

❖ **When you begin to understand that God is a Spirit, then you will start to understand how God speaks to you through His Spirit.**

❖ **When you are born again, renewed with the life of God, you are receptive to God's voice.**

❖ **It is very unusual to hear God's voice audibly.**

❖ **God speaks to you through your inner man a Spiritual voice from deep inside of your heart.**

❖ **When you silence all other voices in your life, your soul and your body, you will cause your environment to be saturated with the presence of God so you can hear His voice.**

If God is a Spirit, and He speaks to you Spirit-to-spirit, what would the result be if you never spend time in the Spirit of God?

_____

_____

_____

_____

_____

_____

_____

❖ **Matthew 4:4** "But He answered and said, 'It is written, 'Man shall not live by bread alone, but by every word that proceeds from the mouth of God.'"

- We must meditate on the Word of God because it feeds our spirit; it is spiritual food.
- Reading God's Word and meditating on it is something that you should do daily.

❖ <u>**John 6:63**</u> "It is the Spirit who gives life; the flesh profits nothing. The words that I speak to you are spirit, and they are life."

❖ <u>**John 6:51**</u> "I am the living bread which came down from Heaven. If anyone eats of this bread, he will live forever; and the bread that I shall give is My flesh, which I shall give for the life of the world."

- Allow your mind to be transformed and let it be renewed by the Word of God.

- Meditate on the truth and absorb it into your life. You renew your mind by the Word of God.
- Allow your spirit to rule over your body, so you do not give in to the works of the flesh.
- If you want to walk closer to God, understand that the spirit of man and the Spirit of God are one.
- The Holy Spirit will reveal to you the Father's heart. He will take that which is Spiritual and give it to you, but you must receive it from your spirit deep inside your heart.

If you did *not* allow your mind to be transformed and renewed by the Word of God, what would the results be?

_____

_____

_____

_____

_____

_____

_____

❖ **<u>Romans 12:2-3</u>** "And do not be conformed to this world, but be transformed by the renewing of your mind, that you may prove what is that good and acceptable and perfect will of God. For I say, through the grace given to me, to everyone who is among you, not to think of himself more highly than he ought to think, but to think soberly, as God has dealt to each one a measure of faith."

- The things that you encounter in this earthly realm can be so contrary to what the Spirit of God is speaking over you from the Heavenly realms.
- The truth from Heaven is the true reality in your life.
- On earth, your mind, will, and emotions must be transformed by the renewing of your mind by the Word of God.
- Only when your mind is renewed can you start to have a framework whereby you can hear what the Holy Spirit is saying to you.
- You need to have the revelation and understanding of how much God loves you.
- You must let the realm of the Holy Spirit dominate your life.

How can you allow the realm of the Holy Spirit to dominate your life?

_____

_____

_____

_____

_____

_____

_____

❖ **John 15:26** (AMP) "But when the Helper (Comforter, Advocate, Intercessor-Counselor, Strengthener, Standby) comes, whom I will send to you from the Father, that is the Spirit of Truth who comes from the Father, He will testify and bear witness about Me."

- The Holy Spirit is the Spirit of Truth who proceeds from the Father, and He will testify according to what the Father says about Jesus.
- The Holy Spirit is the third person of the Holy Trinity.
- The same Holy Spirit who hovered over the waters at the creation of the world is inside of you.
- The Holy Spirit in you is your: Comforter, your Advocate, your Counselor, Your Strengthener, and your Standby.
- The Holy Spirit will testify and bear witness about Jesus.

THE COMFORTER

- ❖ God's plan for you is much greater than you are grasping right now.
- ❖ The Holy Spirit comforts you when you are looking at your circumstances. He is telling you that everything is going to work out, just believe.
- ❖ You will be astounded at how fast things change, and God comes through for you.
- ❖ When the victory is yours, you will see that the Holy Spirit was calling things that are not as though they were.
- ❖ "God, who gives life to the dead and calls those things which do not exist as though they did (Romans 4:17)."
- ❖ While you were looking at your circumstance, God was working things out for your good.
- ❖ "And we know that all things work together for good to those who love God, to those who are called according to His purpose (Romans 8:28)."
- ❖ "Yet in all these things we are more than conquerors through Him who loved us (Romans 8:37)."
- ❖ Receive Him as your comforter, and you will start to hear the voice of God.

In what life circumstances have you not been able to receive the Holy Spirit as your comforter but would like to? Take time right now to pray and receive Him as your comforter.

_____

_____

_____

_____

_____

THE COUNSELOR

- ❖ You need the wisdom and the understanding of God to implement the will of God into your life.
- ❖ The Holy Spirit counsels you by giving you advice; it is like getting legal advice from the voice of God.
- ❖ When you do not know what to do deep inside of you is the Counselor, and He can tell you what to do.
- ❖ Remember, God speaks to you in your spirit, and you receive it into your spirit. Your understanding causes you to act in the flesh, but it must first be spiritually discerned.

What could be the result of *not* consulting the Holy Spirit when you require counsel, wisdom, and understanding on an important matter?

_____

_____

_____

_____

_____

THE HELPER

- ❖ The Helper will implement what is being said by God and helps you in your weaknesses when you do not know what to do.
- ❖ The Helper inside of you takes what is spiritual and gives it to you so that it can be carried out in your life.
- ❖ After you gain understanding from the Helper than what is in Heaven can come into this realm through your understanding.
- ❖ Part of God's voice is a physical manifestation of what you hear and understand.
- ❖ You have not been left an orphan but have received the Spirit of adoption.
- ❖ "For you did not receive the spirit of bondage again to fear, but you received the Spirit of adoption by whom we cry out, "Abba, Father (Romans 8:15)."

Are you ready to ask the Holy Spirit to help you when you do not know what to do? What do you think will happen when He takes what is spiritual and gives it to you?

_____

_____

_____

_____

_____

THE ADVOCATE

- ❖ The Advocate will represent you when you do not know what to pray the Holy Spirit helps you in your weaknesses.

- ❖ "Likewise the Spirit also helps in our weaknesses. For we do not know what we should pray for as we ought, but the Spirit Himself makes intercession for us with groanings which cannot be uttered (Romans 8:26)."
- ❖ The Holy Spirit takes hold of you, and you pray out the will of God.
- ❖ You must always pray in the Spirit yielding to the Holy Spirit to speak forth mysteries in your unknown language; they are His perfect prayers.

What will happen when you yield to the Holy Spirit and speak in your unknown language?

_____

_____

_____

_____

_____

THE STRENGTHENER

- ❖ "But if the Spirit of Him who raised Jesus from the dead dwells in you, He who raised Christ from the dead will also give life to your mortal bodies through His Spirit who dwells in you (Romans 8:11)."
- ❖ The same power that rose Jesus from the dead is dwelling in you, and that awesome power is the Holy Spirit.
- ❖ That same Holy Spirit will cause life to come into your mortal body and ignite your spirit.
- ❖ The Strengthener will help your mind to align with the will of God.
- ❖ You will gain understanding because He strengthens you from inside of your spirit.
- ❖ You must hand over your will and yield to Him.
- ❖ The Holy Spirit is saying to you to be strong in the Lord and His mighty power (see Ephesians 6:10).

With what power does the Holy Spirit strengthen you? What happens when your mind aligns with the will of God?

_____

_____

_____

_____

_____

_____

_____

THE STANDBY

❖ **<u>Genesis 1:3</u>** "And the Spirit of God was hovering over the face of the waters."

- The Holy Spirit hovered over the waters in Genesis, and He hovers over your life and spirit right now.
- The Standby is ready to execute whatever commands God sends from His throne in Heaven to you.
- The Holy Spirit is the communicator between the angels of God and you.
- When the Father says something, then things written about you must come to pass, the angels are notified and sent on your behalf.
- The Standby Holy Spirit ignites your spirit to cause you to speak what God wants you to say.
- When you obey, you will speak forth by the Spirit of Prophecy.
- The Holy Spirit is hovering over the face of your life right now, and He wants to create things in your life.

In what ways can you yield to the Holy Spirit so that He can execute the commands of God for your life?

_____

_____

_____

_____

_____

_____

_____

_____

_____

_____

_____

DR. KEVIN L. ZADAI

CHAPTER 5

The Breath of God

"Jesus answered and said to Him, 'Most assuredly, I say to you, unless one is born again, he cannot see the kingdom of God.'" John 3:3

❖ **John 3:4-8** "Nicodemus said to Him, 'How can a man be born when he is old? Can he enter a second time into his mother's womb and be born?' Jesus answered, 'Most assuredly, I say to you, unless one is born of water and the Spirit, he cannot enter the kingdom of God. That which is born of the flesh is flesh, and that which is born of the Spirit is spirit. Do not marvel that I said to you, 'You must be born again.' The wind blows where it wishes and you hear the sound of it, but you cannot tell where it comes from and where it goes. So is everyone who is born of the Spirit.'"

- When the wind blows, you do not see the wind, but you do see the effects of the wind. You see the trees swaying in the wind, and Jesus says that is the way the Spirit works in us.
- You do not see the Spirit of God, but you see the effects of the Spirit.
- You have been given everything that you need for life and godliness. Through God's promises, you can be a partaker of the divine nature.

❖ **2 Peter 1:4** "By which have been given to us exceedingly great and precious promises, that through these you may be partakers of the divine nature, having escaped the corruption that is in the world through lust."

- You must back out of the voices of the world.
- Tell your soul to be quiet so that your spirit, which is filled with the Holy Spirit, can be heard.

❖ **John 20:22** "And when He had said this, He breathed on them, and said to them, 'Receive the Holy Spirit.'"

- Jesus breathed on His disciples to receive the Holy Spirit, and His breath was the same breath as the Holy Spirit.
- The breath of life that God breathed into man (see Genesis 2:7) is the same breath that God breathed into you when you became born again, and you came alive.
- This same breath is breathed on you when you receive the Holy Spirit and speak in other tongues. God's breath is life.

What voices in the world is the Holy Spirit telling you to back away from?

_____

_____

_____

_____

_____

_____

❖ **Ezekiel 37:8-10** (AMP) "And I looked and behold, there were sinews on the bones, and flesh grew and skin covered them; but there was no breath in them. Then said He to me, 'Prophesy to the breath, son of man, and say to the breath,' thus says the Lord God: 'Come from the four winds, O breath, and breathe on these slain, that they may live.' So I prophesied as He commanded me, and the breath came into them, and they came to life and stood up on their feet, an exceedingly great army."

- God can speak to you in different ways, and it does not have to be in words necessarily.

❖ **Acts 2:4** "And they were filled with the Holy Spirit and began to speak with other tongues, as the Spirit gave them utterance."

- When you prophesy, you are speaking as the Spirit gives you utterance.
- You are speaking from the spirit realm originating in Heaven.
- The Spirit of Prophecy is the testimony of Jesus Christ.

❖ **John 4:24** "God is Spirit and those who worship Him must worship in spirit and truth."

- God's voice is activated inside your spirit.
- God is a Spirit, and those who worship Him must worship in spirit and truth, His Spirit to your spirit.
- A prophet allows God's voice to speak through them, and they speak God's Word forth.
- When you speak forth, you should speak as the very oracles of God.

❖ **1 Peter 4:11** "If anyone speaks, let him speak as the oracles of God. If anyone ministers, let him do it as with the ability which God supplies, that in all things God may be glorified through Jesus Christ, to whom belong the glory and the dominion forever and ever. Amen."

- When you speak forth, you should speak as the very oracles of God."
- Paul said that you should desire to prophesy, especially. He would rather you prophesy than anything else because it edifies the church (see 1 Corinthians 14:1).
- If you are born again and baptized in the Holy Spirit, you can speak in tongues and ask God for the interpretation of what you are saying.
- The Holy Spirit wants to speak through you more than you know.
- If the resurrection power that raised Jesus from the dead is dwelling in you, then that same power is going to quicken your mortal body.
- Do not limit the Holy Spirit of God.
- The resurrection power in you is to do God's will. You will raise people from the dead, heal the sick, drive out devils, speak in new tongues, preach and testify of Jesus wherever you go.

How have you limited the resurrection power of the Holy Spirit in you? What would happen if the limitations were removed?

_____

_____

_____

_____

_____

_____

DISCUSSION:

The Holy Spirit is always speaking and always wanting to do God's will on the earth. The problem we are having is that we are waiting for something to happen as a sign for us to do something. We are looking for a physical sign for something that is actually initiated by the voice of God inside of us. The Spirit of God is always speaking, and God wants to do so much through us, and even exceedingly more than we can think or ask (see Ephesians 3:20). You must pray out the mysteries of God and stop waiting for God to move. God is already moving inside of you, and you must put yourself in motion by faith in Him. He lives inside of you. At the pool of Bethesda, a paralytic man was waiting for the water to stir, if he could get into the water ahead of everyone else, he would be healed. He explained to Jesus that he had waited for twenty-eight years for someone to put him into the pool. He never discerned who he was talking to and what Jesus could do for him. Jesus told me that this is what His church is doing today. We are waiting for the water to stir because we might get healed. There are things that God is telling you in your heart that you know will happen but have not happened yet. You must discern that the breath of God is already speaking inside of you with the power that can raise the dead. The same breath that Ezekiel experienced is the same breath of God that is inside of you.

❖ **1 Corinthians 15:42-45** "So also is the resurrection of the dead. The body is sown in corruption, it is raised in incorruption. It is sown in dishonor, it is raised in glory. It is sown in weakness, it is raised in power. It is sown a natural body, it is raised a spiritual body. There is a natural body, and there is a spiritual body. And so it is written, 'The first man Adam became a living being.' The last Adam became a life-giving spirit.'"

- When the first man Adam was created, he was breathed into, and he became alive. Adam became a living soul.
- The last Adam, Jesus Christ, is a life-giving Spirit, so He is continual.
- Jesus is the last Adam, and there will not be another.
- Jesus is a perpetual, continual, life-giving Spirit.
- The life-giving Spirit, the Holy Spirit, is inside of you and He is speaking to you.
- He is forming words inside of you, and you need to speak them out.

❖ **Every believer should prophesy. Moses wished that his whole camp would prophesy (see Numbers 11:29).**

❖ **You do have the voice of God inside of you, and you need to stop waiting for Him to speak and start yielding to the Spirit of God.**

In what ways have you been waiting for God to move when God has been waiting for you to move?

_____

_____

_____

_____

_____

_____

_____

❖ **John 4:23-24** "But the hour is coming, and now is, when the true worshippers will worship the Father in spirit and truth; for the Father is seeking such to worship Him, God is Spirit, and those who worship Him must worship in spirit and truth."

- When you pray in the Spirit, you are accessing the supernatural in your spirit.
- As soon as you put words to what is in the Spirit, it becomes a transaction into this realm. A supernatural event has now come into this physical realm.
- You are taking something that you cannot see, and you are making it physical. You are bringing it into the physical realm, and now it is a supernatural event.

- Praying in tongues and prophesying is so important. As you practice yielding to the Spirit of God, you will begin to speak out according to the Spirit.
- Out of your mouth will come God's thoughts towards you and His plans for your future.
- Your future will become your now, and you will not worry about your future. The transaction is coming from God's Heavenly realm into this natural realm.

❖ **The Spirit of God is the Breath of the Almighty.**

❖ **You are a spirit and was formed as a spirit first and put into a body in your mother's womb.**

❖ **Your soul—your mind, will, and emotions were given to complement and hold together your body and your spirit. Without your body, you cannot be in this earth.**

❖ **Your mind, will, and emotions need to be transformed and side with the Holy Spirit inside of you. You transform your mind by renewing it in the Word of God.**

❖ **"And do not be conformed to this world, but be transformed by the renewing of your mind, that you may prove what is that good and acceptable and perfect will of God (Romans 12:2-3)."**

DR. KEVIN L. ZADAI

CHAPTER 6

The Hidden Man of the Heart

"If then you were raised with Christ, seek those things which are above, where Christ is, sitting at the right hand of God. Set your mind on things above, not on things on the earth." Colossians 3:1-2

DISCUSSION:

God is excited for you to walk with Him and hear His voice; however, it is not about getting God's voice to be louder. Jesus Himself told me that His voice is loud, but the problem is that all the other voices are louder. He told me that you need to tune down and turn off a lot of the other voices in your life to hear His voice. God is speaking to your inner man who is in your heart. Many people misunderstand and are waiting for God to speak to them either audibly, or through their circumstances or other ways. You might not ever hear God speak to you audibly in your entire life. You may be completely faithful to God your whole life on earth and never see Jesus or hear Him audibly. I was told not to teach on these outward circumstances but to teach you that Jesus speaks to your heart, your spirit, and He speaks loudly. There are many voices in the world and many bad voices that people misunderstand or misinterpret.

❖ **2 Corinthians 11:14** "And no wonder! For satan himself transforms himself into an angel of light."

- There are evil spirits who are familiar with you, your circumstances, and your family, and they can follow you around for a long time.

- These spirits speak and interject into your life, and it can sound like God, but it is a total deception.
- I am telling you this so that you are not deceived.
- Jesus loves you so much, and you are not rejected.
- You are adopted into the blood, and God has amazing plans for you.

❖ **Mark 16:17-18** "And these signs will follow those who believe: In My name they will cast out demons; they will speak with new tongues; they will take up serpents; and if they drink anything deadly, it will by no means hurt them; they will lay hands on the sick, and they will recover."

- You do not have to look for all kinds of outward signs and manifestations. Signs will *follow* those who believe.
- God does the signs and wonders, and you do the believing. As you do your part, God will do His part.

What are some things that the Holy Spirit is asking you to believe for from your Heavenly Father that seems impossible?

_____

_____

_____

_____

_____

_____

_____

_____

_____

❖ God wants to speak to you, but He might not speak to you like the Old Testament prophets who heard an audible voice. God is now dwelling within you by His Holy Spirit. You have a giant receiver in you that can hear God's voice. The frequency is already tuned to hear His voice being broadcast loudly from Heaven. You must tune out the other voices you are listening to and tune into Heaven to receive.

- God may not tell you exactly what you are supposed to do tomorrow. He might be asking you to trust Him by going to church tomorrow to be there and serve Him.
- God may want you to go out and love on someone as you go about your day or do something for someone.
- God says that if you take care of His people, then He will take care of you.
- "He who is gracious and lends a hand to the poor lends to the Lord, And the Lord will repay him for his good deed (Proverbs 19:17 AMP)."
- Go out and feed the poor, share with people, and give of yourself, and sometimes God will speak to you on the way.

❖ **You have a receiver in you, and it is already set up for you to receive God's voice.**

❖ **There is nothing hidden from you inside your spirit.**

❖ **God has already anointed you, and you can flow with God inside your spirit.**

❖ **There is no need to look for outward signs anymore.**

❖ **Matthew 6:33** "But seek first the Kingdom of God and His righteousness, and all these things shall be added to you."

- You do not even have to pray for yourself because God said that He would supply all your needs (see Philippians 4:19). Pray for others and see what God will do.
- Let the Holy Spirit speak to you about other people. Yield in your spirit and pray the prayers of God for others, and move with the Holy Spirit of God.
- If you want this move of the Spirit, it is already happening, and you cannot wait any longer.
- The Holy Spirit wants to talk to you, but it is about other people, and it is about the environment around you.
- "Do not forget to entertain strangers, for by so doing some have unwittingly entertained angels (Hebrews 13:2)."
- Unleash yourself from the way religion has taught you. God is speaking to you and telling you to go forth and not to wait.

❖ **The only day that Jesus told the people of God to *wait* was on the day of Pentecost when they were to receive the Holy Spirit. Ever since that day, the waiting is over.**

- The Holy Spirit wants to take over your life if you let Him.
- You want God to speak to you, but He may want to speak *through you* to the lost and hurting.
- We need to go forth and speak forth.
- When you go out to minister that flow of the Holy Spirit goes out to others through you. As it is happening your spirit is being supplied food from Heaven to supply food for others.
- Remember that flesh is flesh, and you cannot look for God to speak to your flesh because He is Spirit.

The Holy Spirit is asking you to go forth; the waiting is over. Write a plan for yourself to go forth this week and start to minister the work of the kingdom on earth.

_____

_____

_____

_____

_____

_____

_____

- ❖ **1 Corinthians 9:27** "But I discipline my body and bring it into submission, lest, when I have preached to others, I myself should become disqualified."

  - You must say no to your body daily.
  - Allow the Word of God to be stronger in your life than your mind, will, and emotions.
  - Renew your mind with the Word of God (see Romans 12:2).

- ❖ **Philippians 1:19-25** "For I know that this will turn out for my deliverance through your prayer and the supply of the Spirit of Jesus Christ, according to my earnest expectation and hope that in nothing I shall be ashamed, but with all boldness, as always, so now also Christ will be magnified in my body, whether by life or by death. For to me, to live is Christ, and to die is gain. But if I live on in the flesh, this will mean fruit from my labor; yet what I shall choose I cannot tell. For I am hard-pressed between the two, having a desire to depart and be with Christ, which is far better. Nevertheless to remain in the flesh is more needful for you."

- You can have this attitude where you would rather go and be with the Lord, but you choose to stay to help others.
- You will begin to understand that as you live on in the flesh that your life is not your own anymore. You will begin to live for Christ and die to self.
- Paul's revelation can be transferred to us through this Scripture from his jail cell. Our lives can change because Paul chose to write this according to what was revealed to him, and not from out of his circumstances.
- To some Christians today, Paul may not have looked successful. He spent a large part of his life in jail, and he did not even own a house or have a mode of transportation. Paul had to ask for parchment and outer garments, yet his letters have inspired the world for generations.
- Stop looking for outward signs and stop looking for God to speak to you from outside of yourself. Your human spirit has already been activated by the born again experience, and God's voice is already inside of you by the Holy Spirit.

❖ **On earth, we must live from out of our spirit, and not from out of our circumstances.**

What circumstances have occupied your mind and stopped you from hearing God's voice?

_____

_____

_____

_____

_____

_____

❖ **2 Corinthians 4:16-18** "Therefore we do not lose heart. Even though our outward man is perishing, yet the inward man is being renewed day by day. For our light affliction, which is but for a moment, is working for us a far more exceeding and eternal weight of glory, while we do not look at the things which are seen, but at the things which are not seen. For the things which are seen are temporary, but the things which are not seen are eternal."

❖ **2 Corinthians 5:1-8** "For we know that if our earthly house, this tent, is destroyed, we have a building from God, a house not made with hands, eternal in the Heavens. For in this we groan, earnestly desiring to be clothed with our habitation which is from Heaven, if indeed, having been clothed, we shall not be found naked. For we who are in this tent groan, being burdened, not because we want to be unclothed, but further clothed, that mortality may be swallowed up by life. Now He who has prepared us for this very thing is God, who also has given us the Spirit as a guarantee. So we are always confident, knowing that while we are at home in the body we are absent from the Lord. For we walk by faith, not by sight. We are confident, yes, well pleased rather to be absent from the body and to be present with the Lord."

- While we are in the body, this is not our true habitation.
- Our true habitation is a body that was given in the resurrection.
- In the Lord, we are actually in Heaven in our spirit.
- We are just visiting here, and our body is like a temporary tent that we are using while we are on earth.
- Our permanent home is in Heaven, where we only hear the one true voice, and that voice is God's.
- You have one parent, and His name is Father God Jehovah, the Most High, seated on His throne.
- You were sent to earth, you are just visiting, and this is not your home.
- Your Father always speaks to you because He has adopted you.
- God has already spoken into your life and has written books about you.

❖ **Whatever you will do on this earth has already been written about you, and you just have to agree with God for it.**

❖ **On this earth, everything you do in the flesh is by faith. When we walk on this earth, we walk by faith and not by sight.**

- Seek God's face; it is not complicated but easy.
- Stop looking for signs
- You already have a direct line to God.

❖ **<u>Romans 8:37</u>** "Yet in all these things we are more than conquerors through Him who loved us."

- You can go forth and conquer because it is all yours, and the limits are off.
- You cannot fail.

❖ **<u>Romans 8:1</u>** "There is therefore now no condemnation to those who are in Christ Jesus, who do not walk according to the flesh, but according to the Spirit."

- Your past is destroyed, so do not bother to look back.

❖ **<u>Exodus 23:22</u>** "But if you indeed obey His voice and do all that I speak, then I will be an enemy to your enemies and an adversary to your adversaries."

- Your enemies are now God's enemies, and your adversaries are now His adversaries.

What is the Holy Spirit telling you to do differently in your life knowing that you are just visiting the earth in a temporary body, and your true habitation is with your Father in Heaven?

_____

_____

_____

_____

_____

_____

_____

- **2 Corinthians 5:16-18** "Therefore, from now on, we regard no one according to the flesh. Even though we have known Christ according to the flesh, yet now we know Him thus no longer. Therefore, if anyone is in Christ, he is a new creation; old things have passed away; behold, all things become new."

  - We do not know anyone according to the flesh anymore. God speaks Spiritually to us.

What is wrong with knowing someone "after the flesh"?

_____

_____

_____

_____

_____

_____

_____

❖ **Ephesians 2:6** (NLT) "For He raised us from the dead along with Christ and seated us with Him in the Heavenly realms because we are united with Christ Jesus."

- We are seated in Heavenly realms with Christ Jesus.
- Our spirit man is seated at the right hand of God even now.

❖ **Colossians 3:1-2** "If you were raised with Christ, seek those things which are above, where Christ is, sitting at the right hand of God. Set your mind on things above, not on things on the earth."

- You were raised with Christ seek the things which are from Heaven.
- Do not set your mind on things on the earth but set your mind on things above.

❖ **Revelation 3:21** "To him who overcomes I will grant to sit with Me on My throne, as I also overcame and sat down with My Father on His throne."

- He who overcomes will sit with the Most Holy, and the Most Holy speaks inside of you.

❖ **The voice of God is speaking loud inside your spirit right now. If you want to hear God's voice, it is as easy as turning down all the other voices in your life.**

CHAPTER 7

Your Mind, Will, and Emotions

"Now may the God of Peace Himself sanctify you completely; and may your whole spirit, soul, and body be preserved blameless at the coming of our Lord Jesus Christ." 1 Thessalonians 5:23

DISCUSSION:

You are made up of three parts; your soul, your spirit, and your body. Your soul is a part of you, but it is not the real you. The hidden man of the heart, your spirit is the real you. When you are ready to leave this earthly body, I call it your *earth suit*, it is your spirit that will go on to Heaven. Your spirit will live eternally with the Father and Jesus in the Heavenly realms, and that is the real you. Your soul is where your mind, will, and emotions are. When you are born again, your spirit becomes right with God, but your soul and your body will not cooperate unless you make them. Your soul and your body are like children who must be disciplined. Your soul — your mind, will, and emotions want to do what they want to do, but your spirit is saying, "But God!" Your mind, will, and emotions can be redeemed, but it is done by the transforming and renewing of your mind by the Holy Spirit and the Word of God. "And do not be conformed to this world, but be transformed by the renewing of your mind, that you may prove what is that good and acceptable and perfect will of God (Romans12:2)." Your soul can cause you to have emotions that are not based in fact. You could feel rejected even if you were never rejected. Your soul could tell you that everyone is looking at you when no one is looking at you. Feelings can lie to you, but your spirit will tell you the truth.

❖ **1 Corinthians 13:11** (AMP) "When I was a child, I talked like a child, I thought like a child, I reasoned like a child; when I became a man, I did away with childish things."

- Your soul needs to be developed and matured because your spirit is born again, but your soul is not.
- Do you wonder why you sabotage yourself? Paul said that there are people who oppose themselves within themselves (see 2 Timothy 2:25 KJV).
- David told his soul to find hope in God when it was disquieted (see Psalm 42:5). David's spirit man was talking to his soul and telling it to settle down. He was encouraging himself in the Lord.
- When David faced the giant, he was speaking out of his spirit when he prophesied that Goliath dared to defy the armies of the living God (see 1 Samuel 17:26). He was not speaking out of his emotions but from the voice of God, knowing he could not be defeated.
- Unfortunately, many people today are reacting out of their emotions just as King Saul and his army were doing that day by hiding in their tents afraid of the giant.

In what areas of your life have you been reacting out of your emotions and not out of trust in your Heavenly Father to work things out for your good?

_____

_____

_____

_____

_____

_____

_____

_____

❖ **1 Corinthians 14:2** (AMP) "For one who speaks in an unknown tongue does not speak to people but to God; for no one understands him or catches his meaning, but by the Spirit he speaks mysteries [secret truths, hidden things] not obvious to the understanding."

- Paul is giving us the secret of how to overcome our soul by living in the Spirit and hearing Gods voice.
- There is a transaction from the spiritual realm to this physical realm in order for you to overcome your soul.
- David responded out of his spirit and not out of his soul, which was his mind, will, and emotions.
- What Paul is saying here is that the Holy Spirit is overriding and bypassing your soul and speaking the truth to your spirit.
- The hidden things here are not obvious to your understanding but have already been deposited into your spirit.
- You do not understand what you are saying in tongues because your spirit is speaking with God and bypassing your soul.
- If you walk in the Spirit and want to hear God's voice and God is a Spirit, He will speak to you Spirit-to-spirit.
- God will bypass your mind, so do not wait to hear Him in your mind, body, or circumstances.

How has your mind, will, or emotions worked against you to try to prevent you from speaking in tongues?

_____

_____

_____

_____

_____

_____

❖ God speaks to you, and you speak to your circumstances. You are the ambassador to the kingdom of God on the earth, and you are in authority here on earth. You are on earth legally in your earth suit because you were born through your mother's womb. satan is on earth because he took earth over in conquest when he deceived Adam and Eve in the garden. The god of this world is satan, according to Paul (see 2 Corinthians 4:4), but we have authority over him through Jesus Christ. God has given us the Holy Spirit to talk to God with tongues. Speaking in tongues causes you to pray perfect prayers to bring to earth the will of God for your life and others. We are to be busy telling people about Jesus. We need to be teaching and admonishing each other, which will bring us all to the unity of the faith. We need to become one with purpose and serving God in fullness with everyone built up in Christ. Let us be about our Fathers work in Christ Jesus. "And He said to them, 'Why did you seek Me? Did you not know that I must be about My Father's business (Luke 2:49).'"

❖ **1 Thessalonians 5:23-24** "Now may the God of peace Himself sanctify you completely; and may your whole spirit, soul, and body be preserved blameless at the coming of our Lord Jesus Christ. He who calls you is faithful, who also will do it."

- Paul names the three parts of our body and tells us that God Himself will sanctify us completely and is faithful to do it for us.
- We must allow the Spirit of God through the Word of God to transform our souls so that our souls do not work against us.

DISCUSSION:

The Lord told me that many people do not enter into the supernatural because their soul is not healed. People's souls are not siding with their spirit, and they need to realize who they are and what has been done for them through Christ Jesus. They need to see how Jesus sees them, how people in Heaven see them, and see that they need to be healed. The way people think about themselves is so foreign from the way people in Heaven think about them. People in Heaven think of you in this generation as heroes. Everyone in Heaven wants to meet you because you were chosen for this end time. Those in Heaven were the ones who started the race and ever since then the race has been going on for generation after generation. We are nearing the end where the culmination of all things will happen. They are looking at us as heroes, and we are sitting here feeling rejected, hurt, lonely, and still dealing with past sins. If you went before an earthly judge and he told you that you were not guilty, would you keep coming back to see if it was still true? The Judge would throw you out because he is so busy. You have been forgiven by the blood of Jesus, and it is finished. Do not listen to your mind, will, and emotions if they are not siding with the Lord. Heaven is cheering you on, so get back in the race.

What area of your soul—your mind, will, and emotions, is the Holy Spirit showing you that is not siding with the Holy Spirit within you? Ask God to forgive you by the blood of His Son Jesus and heal those broken areas.

_____

_____

_____

_____

_____

_____

❖ It is time to turn on the devil and make him realize that you know who you are in Christ, Jesus. You are not a victim anymore, and now when you wake up in the morning, the devil is the one who will worry about what you will do today. When you start walking with Jesus in authority and power knowing who you are in Christ then tomorrow, the devil will not be around anymore because he cannot push your buttons anymore. He goes to look for someone who will listen to him and someone who he can influence.

- When you know how to enter into God's rest, it makes the enemy very nervous. You no longer have to live your life out of your own emotions and will.

- When you pray in tongues, it is an encoded language, and the enemy does not understand it. It is between you and God, and it is a great benefit to you to speak in tongues every day.

❖ **Hebrews 4:11-13** (AMP) "Let us therefore make every effort to enter that rest [of God, to know and experience it for ourselves], so that no one will fall by following the same example of disobedience [as those who died in the wilderness]. For the word of God is living and active and full of power [making it operative, energizing, and effective]. It is sharper than any two-edged sword, penetrating as far as the division of the soul and the spirit [the completeness of a person], and of both joints and marrow [the deepest parts of nature], exposing and judging the very thoughts and intentions of the heart. And not a creature exists that is concealed from His sight, but all things are open and exposed, and revealed to the eyes of Him with whom we have to give account."

- As you can see here, the soul and the spirit are listed as two separate things.
- Jesus showed me that His Word is the Spirit of God who divides. When the Word of God comes in, it discerns between the soul and the spirit.
- Jesus told me that if you want to hear His voice, the Word of God will separate between the soul and the spirit. Your soul is in you, but the real you is your spirit and Jesus by the Holy Spirit is dwelling in there with you.

- The real you knows God and has no doubts or fears.
- Your spirit knows that you will not only survive this life, but you will thrive in this life by the power of God working in you.
- Your spirit knows that you cannot lose and wants to take the land, and the devils are letting go and fleeing.

Why is the Word of God so important, and what does it accomplish in your soul and spirit?

_____

_____

_____

_____

_____

_____

❖ **The Lord says that you are worth more than you know, and you are not a victim. God has caused you to be more than a conqueror, and it is in your inner man where you must first realize that truth.**

CHAPTER 8

Praying in the Spirit

"And they were all filled with the Holy Spirit and began to speak with other tongues, as the Spirit gave them utterance." Acts 2:4

DISCUSSION:

God wants to heal your body and your soul. Your spirit was already healed when you confessed that Jesus Christ is Lord. You cannot let your soul drag you down, which is the reason why you must discipline your soul. Did you ever take someone along with you somewhere and you felt as though you were dragging them around all day? You think to yourself how you are never going to bring them with you again. It is like dragging someone with you who does not want to go with you. Your soul will be that way with you, and so will your body. When you pray in the Spirit, in tongues, it overthrows your soul. Your soul throws a fit because it cannot participate in the supernatural event of praying in the Spirit. Your body and soul will fight you every time you go to pray in tongues. As you discipline your body and soul by praying this way, you will begin to enjoy overthrowing the demonic. You can truly be glad that you are born again, separated out, translated into the kingdom of light and not a part of this world. The demons hate when you speak in tongues, when you use the name of Jesus, and when you talk about the blood of Jesus. Praying in tongues infuriates the devil, and it is a powerful weapon of your warfare. When you pray in tongues, the devil is left out, your soul is left out, and your body is left out. You are then free to be and operate in who you are in the Spirit of God. "For the

Lord is the Spirit; and wherever the Spirit of the Lord is, there is freedom (2 Corinthians 3:17 NLT)." In the Spirit of God, you are a prince, a king, and an authority figure on this earth. You are ordained to change the atmosphere of this generation as one by one we walk in what we are called to do. We are called to unify and build up the body of Christ, and praying in tongues is an integral part of walking in God's Spirit.

Why are your soul and body left out when you pray in tongues?

_____

_____

_____

_____

_____

❖ **1 Corinthians 14:14-15** (AMP) "For if I pray in a tongue, my spirit prays, but my mind is unproductive [because it does not understand what my spirit is praying]. Then what am I to do? I will pray with the spirit [by the Holy Spirit that is within me] and I will pray with the mind [using words I understand]; I will sing with the spirit [by the Holy Spirit that is within me] and I will sing with the mind [using words I understand]."

- You can operate in both realms, the Spirit, and the mind.
- When you pray in the Spirit, pray that you can interpret your tongues.
- When you interpret, you can speak out your language, let's say English, for instance, and your mind can be edified.
- When you pray in the Spirit, and you do not interpret your spirit is edified, but your understanding does not comprehend it and is not edified.
- "But you, beloved, building yourselves up in your most holy faith, praying in the Holy Spirit, keep yourselves in the love of God, looking for the mercy of our Lord Jesus Christ unto eternal life (Jude 20)."

Why should you want the Holy Spirit to interpret when you pray in tongues?

_____

_____

_____

_____

_____

_____

_____

❖ **John 7:37-39** "On the last day, that great day of the feast, Jesus stood and cried out, saying, 'If anyone thirsts, let him come to Me and drink. He who believes in Me, as the Scripture has said, out of his heart will flow rivers of living water.' But this He spoke concerning the Spirit, whom those believing in Him would receive; for the Holy Spirit was not yet given, because Jesus was not yet glorified."

- Jesus refers to the Holy Spirit as the river of life.
- John says the Spirit of God is going to well up within you and flow out of you when you pray in tongues.
- You spring forth into eternity by your words through the Spirit of God.
- You must pray in tongues and speak in the Spirit.
- The Holy Spirit will speak out your future through your tongues with interpretation.
- The Holy Fire of God is coming forth out of your spirit, and it is changing peoples lives.
- People need to hear the pure unadulterated Word of God that is an incorruptible seed.

How does praying in tongues help you to hear God's voice?

_____

_____

_____

_____

_____

_____

_____

❖ **John 6:35** "And Jesus said to them, 'I am the bread of life. He who comes to Me shall never hunger, and He who believes in Me shall never thirst.'"

❖ **John 6:53** "Then Jesus said to them, 'Most assuredly, I say to you, unless you eat the flesh of the Son of Man and drink His blood, you have no life in Him.'"

- The Word of God becomes engrafted into you and becomes part of your being.
- When the Word of God becomes part of your being, your spirit man becomes ignited. Your soul then will no longer be able to influence your spirit and will become submitted.
- Your body sees that it also can no longer influence your spirit, so it submits too.
- When this happens your walk with God becomes easier, and you no longer have the troubles you used to have.

❖ **You must be forceful with demonic forces. Do not coddle them but be strong with them, even rough. Tell them what you are going to do to them as David did to Goliath. David told Goliath that he was going to take his head off that day and feed it to the birds. The devil is the god of this world, but God has given you authority over him.**

- ❖ The power of God wants to influence your spirit, your spirit wants to influence your soul, and your soul wants to influence your body. The result will be that all three parts will walk in one accord and unity.

  - Your spirit is already born again by the Holy Spirit of God.
  - You cannot get any more saved then you are right now. You cannot get any more righteous than you are right now. You are a new creation in Christ Jesus.
  - Your soul needs to be renewed. Your body and soul try to catch you up and can try to turn you sideways; they try to tell you that you are a victim when you are a victor.
  - Tell the devil to leave and be forceful and mean it for he is nothing. Remind the devil that Jesus made a show of him openly and triumphed over him on the cross.
  - "When He had disarmed the rulers and authorities [those supernatural forces of evil operating against us], He made a public example of them [exhibiting them as captives in His triumphal procession], having triumphed over them through the cross (Colossians 2:15 AMP)."
  - Tell the devil that the powers of the coming age have defeated him, and he has no authority in your life.

Is the Holy Spirit showing you any area in your body or soul where you need to tell the devil to leave, and forcefully take your God-given authority over him?

_____

_____

_____

_____

_____

_____

- ❖ **<u>Psalm 23:3</u>** "He restores my soul; He leads me in the paths of righteousness For His name's sake."

  - David said that God restored his soul so your soul can be restored.
  - When you enter into His rest, your soul can enter in and be restful too.

- ❖ The Word of God is going to heal you, correct you, and cause you to walk in the supernatural every day. Your spirit is always participating in the supernatural.

  - Your soul and your body need to be told what to do, and they will not do it on their own.
  - Only your spirit knows what to do on its own without guidance.
  - Sometimes you must speak firmly to your body and soul and say, "no." "We are not going to do that ever!"
  - Before you know it, your body and soul will submit to your spirit man. Your Spirit will be telling your body and soul what you need from them, and they will obey.
  - You will begin to do things out of being led by the Spirit of God, and then you are ruling and reigning in the Spirit.
  - There are demons right now hoping that you stay deceived not knowing your authority in Christ Jesus.
  - They quiver to think that you now have the authority to command them.
  - The devil has tried to keep you in victim mode, but you are breaking free.
  - "And you shall know the truth, and the truth shall make you free (John 8:32)."
  - Christians are ordained by God to rule and reign on this earth.

What behavior has your body or soul-influenced you to indulge in that you know is not the will of God for your life? Take this time to repent, and commit to disciplining your body and soul to align with your spirit, the Holy Spirit, and the purposes of God for your life.

_____

_____

_____

_____

_____

_____

❖ <u>**John 3:5-6**</u> "Jesus answered, 'Most assuredly, I say to you, unless one is born of water and the Spirit, he cannot enter the kingdom of God. That which is born of the flesh is flesh, and that which is born of the Spirit is spirit.'"

- We have the Spirit of God in our spirit, and He is ruling and reigning, and our soul is in submission to whatever God says.
- Everything that God says your soul must agree to and your body must not get in the way.

DISCUSSION:

Sometimes you can find yourself between two opinions. Your spirit may be telling you to do something that is of God, but your soul is telling you that you do not need to do it. God is saying, "Go, go, go." but your soul is saying, "I am going to wait on this." Your soul tells you that people will not like you talking about Jesus or hell to them. God is telling you through your spirit to tell this person that Jesus has redeemed them by the blood of His Son Jesus Christ on the cross. It happened to me when my soul talked me out of sharing Christ with someone. I put it off and then before I got a chance to share Christ with them, they died and are gone now. The Spirit of God knew what I needed to do, but my soul talked me out of doing it. Never delay what the Spirit of God is leading you to do. In God's realm, absolute truth reigns, and everything about God is true. Jesus once asked me if I was in or out because if I was out, I needed to step aside because Jesus was going ahead. I used to think that God wanted to do what I want to do, and I found out that I am not in charge, and He is. Now I realize that everything is fine as long as I am doing what the Spirit of God is doing, what Jesus is doing, and what the Father's heart is. If I want to do what I want to do, then I am separating myself from God's plan and purpose. Now my soul is all that I am stuck with because my spirit wants to go and do the things God wants me to do but remember we can discipline our souls.

What has your soul talked you into waiting on, that the Holy Spirit has been encouraging and reminding you to do?

_____

_____

_____

_____

_____

❖ **Galatians 2:20** "I have been crucified with Christ; it is no longer I who live, but Christ lives in me; and the life which I now live in the flesh I live by faith in the Son of God, who loved me and gave Himself for me."

❖ **Matthew 26:41** "Watch and pray, lest you enter into temptation. The spirit indeed is willing, but the flesh is weak."

- Your body is supposed to be crucified with Christ, and it is the only way to get the body to listen to your spirit.

- You must die daily to crucify the flesh.
- You have to tell your flesh that it is not going to do what it wants to do.
- Jesus wanted the disciples to pray because He knew that they did not discern what was about to happen.
- Jesus knew that they were about to fall into temptation because the spirit was willing, but the flesh was weak.
- The Spirit of God is wanting to tell you something, to pray, to yield to the Spirit of God, to crucify the flesh. It is a spiritual matter that you will feel in your flesh.

❖ **Matthew 16:24** "Then Jesus said to His disciples, 'If anyone desires to come after Me, let him deny himself, and take up his cross, and follow Me.'"

- You must live the crucified life.

❖ **1 Corinthians 6:16-20** "Or do you not know that he who is joined to a harlot is one body with her? For 'the two,' He says, 'shall become one flesh.' But he who is joined to the Lord is one spirit with Him. Flee sexual immorality. Every sin that a man does is outside the body, but he who commits sexual immorality sins against his own body. Or do you not know that your body is the temple of the Holy Spirit who is in you, whom you have from God, and you are not your own? For you were bought at a price; therefore glorify God in your body and in your spirit which are God's."

- Your spirit is joined to the Lord, and your body must listen to your spirit.
- Paul said to flee sexual sin because of the influence it will have on you.
- Spiritually you are joined to the Lord, and you should enjoy that union that you have in the Holy Spirit.

❖ **2 Peter 1:3-4** "As His divine power has given to us all things that pertain to life and godliness, through the knowledge of Him who called us by glory and virtue, by which have been given to us exceedingly great and precious promises, that through these you may be partakers of the divine nature, having escaped the corruption that is in the world through lust."

- God does not have a body as we have with flesh and blood. Jesus had a body like ours that the Father worked salvation through on the cross.
- God does not have the same flesh and bone body that we have, but He is saying that we can be partakers of the divine nature. God is saying that it is a spiritual experience that we can have in our earthly body.
- The same Spirit that raised Jesus from the dead is in us and can give life to our mortal bodies (see Romans 8:11).
- God's life inside your body is not going to cause you to sin. His life inside of you is not going to cause you to be weak.
- God's Spirit inside of you is going to quicken your body to cause it to act in unity with your spirit.
- Your mind, will and, emotions and body are folding over and submitting to your spirit.
- Now you are ruling and reigning.

What is the Holy Spirit speaking to you about fleeing sexual immorality or any other lust of the flesh? The Holy Spirit inside of you can quicken your mortal body and cause you to act in unity with your spirit, ask to be a partaker in the divine nature.

_____

_____

_____

_____

_____

- ❖ **Every day when you wake up realize that you are, first of all, a spirit being. You live in a body, and you possess a soul, which is your mind, will, and emotions. Your spirit man has never known defeat and that the Spirit of God is communicating in your spirit the truth about Heaven. Everything written about you in Heaven is accessible by the Spirit.**

- ❖ <u>**1 Corinthians 2:1-10**</u> "And I, brethren, when I came to you, did not come with excellence of speech or of wisdom declaring to you the testimony of God. For I determined not to know anything among you except Jesus Christ and Him crucified. I was with you in weakness, in fear, and in much trembling. And my speech and my preaching were not with persuasive words of human wisdom, but in demonstration of the Spirit and of power, that your faith should not be in the wisdom of men but in the power of God. However, we speak wisdom among those who are mature, yet not the wisdom of this age, nor of the rulers of this age, who are coming to nothing. But we speak the wisdom of God in a mystery, the hidden wisdom which God ordained before the ages for our glory, which none of the rulers of this age knew; for had they known, they would not have crucified the Lord of glory. But as it is written: "Eye has not seen, nor ear heard, nor have entered into the heart of man the things which God has prepared for those who love Him." But God has revealed them to us through His Spirit. For the Spirit searches all things, yes, the deep things of God."

  - The Holy Spirit that is in you is a Spirit of power. The power of the Holy Spirit in you is also the Spirit of revelation.
  - The revelation that the Holy Spirit can access are the mysteries of God.
  - The mysteries of God is the heart of God.
  - The Spirit searches the deep things of God and makes them known to you in your spirit.
  - We have been called to a supernatural life in Christ Jesus to participate and be partakers of the divine nature.

- Why are you allowing your reasoning faculties, your mind, will and emotions to limit you?
- Why are you allowing your body to talk you out of what Jesus is saying to you in your spirit?
- To hear God's voice, you must tell your body it is not going to talk you out of the will of God.
- You must tell your soul to be quiet and then sit in the presence of the Lord and soak in God's presence.
- When you meditate on His Word, God will start to visit you.
- I pray in tongues all the time in my spirit.
- The spirit realm has many more dimensions than our three-dimensional world, so do not limit God.
- God is speaking by His Spirit right now inside of you, and He is telling you the truth and telling you that you can hear His voice.

Write a daily plan that includes a specific time to sit in the presence of the Lord soaking in God's presence, speaking in tongues, and reading and meditating on His Word. Be prepared to begin to hear God's voice and do not limit Him!

_____

_____

_____

_____

_____

_____

_____

_____

_____

l Within

'hen you need to respond."
sked, 'Why do you always speak to
bles?'" Matthew 13:9-10 TPT

, 'You've been given the intimate
iths and mysteries of the realm of
everyone who listens with an open
evelation until he has more than
an open, teachable heart, even the
taken away from them.'"

DISCUSSION:

For this discussion, please read Matthew 13 in The Passion Translation, and it will prepare you for this lesson. In the first parable of chapter 13, Jesus told me that even though it talks about the sower and the seed, that much more time is spent on the different types of soils. Jesus told His disciples that if they understand this parable, then they will understand the deep mysteries of the kingdom of God. These things have been hidden, but they have been given to us by the Spirit of God. Jesus told me that if you look, you will see that the Word of God is the seed, and it is very simple. He told me that the soils represent men's heart's and that each soil is a condition of our hearts. There are four types of soil, and our goal is to become good soil knowing that the Word of God is incorruptible and that it originated in Heaven. The Word of God is a person named Jesus, and the Word of God was written on pages called our bible, and it is supernatural. The bible is a record of everything that God is saying, and it has been watered by the Holy Spirit of God and is ready to germinate to produce a crop. The Spirit of God takes the Word of God and ignites it and causes it to come alive. The seed, which is the Word, must hit good soil to produce a crop, and that soil is men's hearts. You may wonder how this helps you to hear God's voice, and it is because it is a process of becoming stronger in the Lord. Understanding your walk here on earth has everything to do with this parable. Jesus said if you understand this parable, then you will understand everything about the kingdom of God. This parable is about the soils and not the sower. The elements include the beaten path, the rocky soil, the thorns, the good soil, the sower, and the seed.

THE HARD SOIL

- The hard soil is the beaten path. When the seed falls here, people will hear the Word of God but will walk away, not understanding it.
- The seed does not take root because the person fails to understand or grasp the true intent of what God is saying.
- The beaten path and the hardened soil does not produce a crop because the evil one comes and takes it away before it can become rooted.
- It is not what you hear but what you understand.
- The mystery behind the Word of God is the intent of God, and that is what you must grasp.
- Some people are hard-hearted, and that is the condition of their heart. They hear the Word of God, but they do not take it into their hearts and do not grasp its intent.
- You can work on the hard-hearted by telling them how much Jesus loves them.
- You must work until you break through and get to the soft soil that is underneath that hard crusty layer.
- The hard-hearted need to know that they are accepted, loved, and forgiven. Most hard-hearted people have been hurt and need love.

❖ **Jesus told me that if you take care of peoples soils, they are going to start to hear His voice strongly. The Word of God needs to take root in you and your life.**

Is the Holy Spirit showing you anyone in your life, that has a hardened heart, that you can show God's love to? Write down ways that you can show them that they are accepted, loved, and forgiven.

_____

_____

_____

_____

_____

THE ROCKY SOIL

- The rocky soil has to do with our commitment level.
- When people get into trouble or are persecuted the soil becomes rocky. These people lose their joy and fail to produce a crop.
- When the soil is full of rocks, the seed cannot grow.
- Under the anointing people will begin to reject the rocks and the hard places in their lives and come out of it.
- You can help these people by reminding them that they are in this for the long run.
- The rocky hearted person needs to rise to a higher level of commitment, and the rocks need to be removed.
- Jesus told me that they need to believe in Him and trust in Him, and they need their joy back. The joy of the Lord is a healing anointing that will come in to heal them.

How can you tell that the condition of someone's heart is full of stones?

_____

_____

_____

_____

_____

THE THORNY SOIL

- Some peoples lives are full of thorns, and they represent the worries and cares of this life.
- Jesus told me they also represent those attracted to wealth and the love of money more than Him.
- People with this condition of the heart need to get the thorns out of the way by laying their cares down and casting them before Him.
- Jesus will take their cares up, and the peace of God will come into their lives.
- You can minister the peace of God to them by telling them how very secure they are in Christ Jesus.
- They no longer need to worry about this life by casting their cares upon Him. They no longer need to chase money.
- They need to seek the kingdom of God and God's way of doing things in the financial realm.
- They need to know how to have money and not let money have them.

❖ **1 Peter 5:6-7 Therefore, humble yourselves under the mighty hand of God, that He may exalt you in due time, casting all your cares upon Him, for He cares for you.**

What is the Holy Spirit telling you about people who put money before God?

_____

_____

_____

_____

_____

THE GOOD SOIL

- This soil is the only soil that produces a crop.
- Even out of this good soil, some would only produce thirty, some sixty and finally some, one hundredfold.
- Jesus told me that if one hundred people are in a room hearing the Word of God, only twenty-five people will produce a crop.
- There are four soil types, and each type represents twenty-five percent.
- Only twenty-five percent of the seed of the Word of God will fall on good ground and produce a crop.
- Out of those twenty-five people, only eight will produce one hundredfold return based on this parable.
- The good soil is a heart that truly hears and receives the Word of God.

How can you produce a hundredfold return on receiving the Word of God?

_____

_____

_____

_____

_____

❖ The Lord told me that if I want to be more effective in my sowing, than I have to prepare the soil of people's hearts. I rely on the gifts of the Spirit to minister to their hearts with the power of God as I teach the parable of the soils.

❖ When your heart is healed, your soil is healed, and your emotions will then line up with the will of God. When this happens, you will sense that your heart is no longer grieved. You will feel the joy of the Lord and the victory over your circumstances through Christ Jesus. You will know that your soil is ready for the Word of God to produce a crop.

❖ The process of receiving from God and receiving healing has to do with humility. Cultivate sensitivity by humility and admit that you are in need. In prayer, ask God for His mercy, let go of pride and tell God you are hurt or in pain. God wants to heal you and prepare your soil readying it for harvest.

WORSHIP

Whenever you are in a service, block everything out, and worship the one true God. Focus on the throne room, and it is okay to use your imagination, remembering that Isaiah saw the Lord sitting on a throne, high and lifted up (Isaiah 6:1). When you worship, you can bow before Him in humility, and do not worry what other people think, focus on God. God wants you to wait on Him and worship Him. Picture the throne room and everything Isaiah saw there because it is still happening there right now. In your darkest hour, that is happening in God's throne room. If you want to fall on your knees or your face, or dance, feel free to do it. As you worship, you are letting your soil become fertile, and your humility before God will cause God to overcome your weaknesses, and He will heal you.

Ask the Holy Spirit to help you discern what is stopping you from worshipping freely? Take your authority over what is preventing you from openly worshipping God without restraint.

_____

_____

_____

_____

_____

_____

_____

DISCUSSION:

I want to differentiate the ways that God speaks to us. Everyone would love a dream from God that is so clear that when we wake up, we will know exactly what God's will for us is. However, that does not always happen. Everyone would like to hear God's audible voice, and while He does speak this way, it is very rare. Who would not want a prophet dressed in animal skins to come over to their house and say, "Thus saith the Lord." Everyone wants a word in service or see angels that speak to them. I would rather hear God whisper to me in that still small voice. The way that God whispers to us in our inner man is the very common way that God speaks to us. While we would all like exciting, powerful experiences that some people have, it does not happen all the time, and for some people, it will never happen. The Holy Spirit has been given to us, and His voice is very quiet. Sometimes it is just knowing in my spirit the right way to go or not go, like a traffic light that is red or green. Paul once said that it seemed right to him and the Holy Ghost to do something, and this is the way for us too. We know when it seems right with the Holy Ghost in us, and this is the way God can speak to us.

What are the ways that God speaks to us, and what is the most common way that we hear God's voice?

_____

_____

_____

_____

_____

_____

_____

_____

_____

CHAPTER 10

Let God Minister Through You

"There are, it may be, so many kinds of voices in the world, and none of them is without signification." 1 Corinthians 14:10 KJV

DISCUSSION:

Be encouraged that God's voice is speaking loud and clear. We are getting rid of all the voices that are not of God and are eliminating them one by one. We can identify between God's voice, our own voice, and the voice of the devil. Paul said, there are so many kinds of voices in the world, but the point is there is only one true voice. The voice that speaks the truth from Heaven is the voice of God pronounced through the Holy Spirit. It has been pronounced through the angels of the Lord and is being spoken by men and women who are moved by the Holy Ghost to speak forth the truth of God. There are all kinds of voices that are talking to you but only one true voice. Remember that sheep are led not driven and sometimes you need to slow down a little and listen. "My sheep hear My voice, and I know them, and they follow Me (John 10:27)." You do know and hear the voice of God and can differentiate between the voice of reason and the voice of an evil spirit.

❖ **Proverbs 20:27** "The spirit of a man is the lamp of the Lord, searching all the inner depths of his heart."

- Our heart is lit up by the lamp of God, and that is how we are guided.
- When you light up inside, and when you feel the anointing it bears witness within you, in the inner depths of your heart.

❖ **<u>1 Corinthians 5:1-5</u>** "It is actually reported that there is sexual immorality among you, and such sexual immorality as is not even named among the Gentiles-that a man has his father's wife! And you are puffed up, and have not rather mourned, that he who has done this deed might be taken away from among you. For I indeed, as absent in body but present in spirit, have already judged, as though I were present, concerning him who has so done this deed. In the name of our Lord Jesus Christ, when you are gathered together, along with my spirit, with the power of our Lord Jesus Christ, deliver such a one to satan for the destruction of the flesh, that his spirit may be saved in the day of the Lord Jesus."

- Paul said that the congregation was to turn this sexually immoral man out, and over to satan for correction.
- Paul said that even though he would not be there in the congregation in his body that he would be there in spirit when they turned the immoral man out.
- There is so much more in the realm of the Spirit that we could be operating in because we are made in God's image.
- Paul had a voice in the congregation even though he was not there in body.
- Paul had the authority of an apostle.
- In Second Corinthians, we see that this man who was given over for correction was successfully brought back into the congregation after he repented.

❖ Begin to meditate on God's Word and start to learn how to walk in the power of God. You will start to hear God's voice, and then you will become God's authority on the earth.

- Paul had the authority of an apostle.
- Even though Paul was not present there with them, he had authority.

- You have a voice when you are not bodily somewhere.
- God has a voice, and He speaks, but He can also speak through you, and you do not even have to be there.
- When you speak by the Spirit of God, you become the voice of God for someone else.
- You can speak as though you are there with them and transfer the will of God to them.
- You must be careful to discern what you are doing in each situation by the words of your mouth.
- You are responsible for what you say.
- You must be careful not to steer people or manipulate them.

Is the Holy Spirit leading and empowering you to be the voice of God for someone else? You can transfer the will of God to them even if you are not present with them.

_____

_____

_____

_____

_____

_____

_____

_____

❖ **Hearing the voice of God becomes a transference of you receiving from God and then giving it out to others.**

STORY:

I was contacted by someone in India who asked for my help while I was live on Facebook. She told me that as I prayed, something moved from her stomach and started to move around her body. She said that she could see the lump moving around as I prayed and it seemed mad, and she wanted it out. I typed back and told her to tell it to go in the name of Jesus and to tell it that she did not want it anymore and it had to go right now. I waited for her to respond, and she typed back that something was screaming out of her and she could not talk. She asked me to please help her. I told her to hold the screen up to her eyes as I typed out, "You foul lying, devil, this is Kevin from the United States, and I am commanding you to leave her now in Jesus name!" It left her because it saw through her eyes what I had typed. She typed back that it was gone and that she was going to sleep. I looked her up much later and found that she is now an evangelist in India. I did not even have to leave my office, and even though India was thousands of miles away, God's will was done. You can be the voice of God for others and be what they need in the Spirit of God. As a believer, you have more authority than you know. After you have developed your spirit, you have your soul renewed; when you have your body submitted, and you hear God's voice, then you can turn on the devil. You can become a person who can speak forth by the Spirit of God and address and command evil spirits to leave. You will command people's spirits to come back into their bodies, raising them from the dead. You will speak in new tongues and lay hands on the sick and command them to be healed. You will preach the gospel, speak the Word of God, and be the voice of God in someone's life. Once you get to the place where you hear God's voice, so not stop there because there is so much more in the Spirit of God.

- You can stand and address things in the Spirit without ever leaving your house.
- There is no time or distance in the Spirit, and you have no limitations.
- I have been in the Spirit, and I have been translated or transported to somewhere else and returned by the Spirit and it was documented.
- Prayer and the voice of the Lord can become ministry in itself, and you can minister to people without ever leaving home.
- The voice of the Lord is strong and mighty, and it thunders.

❖ <u>**Psalm 29:3-5**</u> **"The voice of the Lord is over the waters; The God of glory thunders; The Lord is over many waters. The voice of the Lord is powerful; The voice of the Lord is full of majesty. The voice of the Lord breaks the cedars, Yes, the Lord splinters the cedars of Lebanon."**

❖ **Jesus told me that in every person, there is a gift, a package, and it is everything they will ever need to accomplish what He has written about them from before they were born.**

❖ **With the purpose and destiny that God has written about you, He also provided all provision for you, and it is inside of you already.**

❖ <u>**Romans 11:29**</u> **(KJV) "For the gifts and calling of God are without repentance."**

- The gifts and calling of God never cease speaking inside of you, and they are part of God's voice.
- They have already been placed in your spirit by God, and they must be accomplished.
- Your gifts and calling are needed by everyone in the body of Christ.
- God has portioned out several gifts as the Spirit of God wills to bring the body into unity and build it up.
- God sets in the church some to be apostles, prophets, pastors, teachers, and evangelists.
- These offices are called the five-fold ministry of the church.

❖ If you are called to be a prophet, God will put you through the training to be a prophet.

- God will unwrap the gifts of the prophet in you.
- These gifts involve, the word of knowledge, the word of wisdom, the gift of prophecy, and the gift of healing or working of miracles.
- If your gift is prophecy, then you need to speak.

Your gifts and callings of God are needed by everyone in the body of Christ. What are the gifts and callings that God has placed in you, and what is the Holy Spirit saying to you about activating them?

_____

_____

_____

_____

_____

_____

_____

❖ **If you want authority on the earth, then you have got to be under authority. Great authority comes with being under authority.**

❖ **You learn to transfer from Heaven, you receive an impartation, you receive an anointing, and you become the voice of God for someone else. There are people on earth waiting for you to come to them, and you are destined to speak to them by the power of the Spirit of God.**

About Dr. Kevin Zadai

Kevin Zadai was called to ministry at the age of ten. He attended Central Bible College in Springfield, Missouri, where he received a Bachelor of Arts in Theology. Later, he received training in missions at Rhema Bible College and currently holds a Th. D. from Primus University. He is currently ordained through Rev. Dr. Jesse and Rev. Dr. Cathy Duplantis. At age thirty-one, during a routine day surgery, he found himself on the "other side of the veil" with Jesus. For forty-five minutes, the Master revealed spiritual truths before returning him to his body and assigning him to a supernatural ministry. Kevin holds a commercial pilot license and has been employed by Southwest Airlines for twenty-nine years as a flight attendant. Dr. Kevin is the Founder and President of Warrior Notes and Warrior Notes School of Ministry. He and his lovely wife, Kathi, reside in New Orleans, Louisiana.

DR. KEVIN L. ZADAI

Salvation Prayer

Lord God,

I confess that I am a sinner. I confess that I need Your Son, Jesus. Please forgive me in His name.

Lord Jesus, I believe You died for me and that You are alive and listening to me now.

I now turn from my sins and welcome You into my heart. Come and take control of my life. Make me the kind of person You want me to be.

Now, fill me with Your Holy Spirit who will show me how to live for You. I acknowledge You before men as my Savior and my Lord.

In Jesus's name. Amen.

If you prayed this prayer, please contact us at: info@kevinzadai.com for more information and material. Go to kevinzadai.com for other exciting ministry materials.

Kevinzadai.com

To enroll in our ministry school, go to: Warriornotesschool.com

COMING SOON: WarriorNotes.TV

Made in the
USA
Columbia, SC